SURVIVOR

The Shackleton Expedition

Jil Fine

HIGH interest books

Children's Press®
A Division of Scholastic Inc.
New York / Toronto / London / Auckland / Sydney
Mexico City / New Delhi / Hong Kong
Danbury, Connecticut

Book Design: Laura Stein and Christopher Logan
Contributing Editor: Matthew Pitt

Photo Credits: Cover © Corbis; pp. 1, 5, 9, 17, 25, 35, 40-48, Back
Cover © Corbis; p. 6 by Erica Clendening; p. 7, 13, 23 by Laura Stein;
p. 4 © Sean Sexton Collection/Corbis; p. 8 © Wolfgang Kaehler/Corbis;
pp. 11, 14, 15, 16, 19, 21, 24, 27, 34, 37, 39 © Royal Geographical
Society, London; p. 28 © Photodisc; p. 32 © Peter Johnson/Corbis

Library of Congress Cataloging-in-Publication Data

Fine, Jil.
The Shackleton expedition / Jil Fine.
  p. cm. — (Survivor)
Includes bibliographical references (p.).
Summary: Recounts the story of Shackleton's dangerous exploration
of Antarctica under harsh conditions.
ISBN 0-516-23904-X (lib. bdg.) — ISBN 0-516-23489-7 (pbk.)
1. Shackleton, Ernest Henry, Sir, 1874–1922—Journeys—
Antarctica—Juvenile literature. 2. Endurance (Ship)—Juvenile
literature. 3. Imperial Trans-Antarctica Expedition (1914–1917)—
Juvenile literature. 4. Antarctica—Discovery and exploration—
Juvenile literature. [1. Shackleton, Ernest Henry, Sir, 1874–1922.
2. Explorers. 3. Endurance (Ship) 4. Imperial Trans-Antarctic
Expedition (1914–1917) 5. Antarctica—Discovery and exploration.]
I. Title. II. Series.

G850 1914 .S53 F56 2002
919.8'904—dc21
                                        2001037276

Contents

Introduction

During a time of great explorers, Sir Ernest Shackleton of England was one of the greatest. Pioneers like Shackleton were the celebrities of their time, much like sports figures and movie stars are now. In 1914, Sir Shackleton led twenty-seven men in an attempt to do what had never been done before—cross the Antarctic continent on foot.

Shackleton had sailed to Antarctica twice before, but nothing could have prepared him for what lay ahead. For more than two years, Shackleton and his crew were trapped in the harshest climate on Earth. Never reaching Antarctica, the men suffered frostbite, exhaustion, and near-starvation. On some days, their strength and hope were barely enough to

Even before his ill-fated attempt to cross Antarctica on foot, Sir Ernest Shackleton was known as a great explorer.

get them through. Over stormy seas, dangerous cliffs, and rivers of ice, the men survived terrible conditions.

Their voyage was one of courage and extreme danger. The story of the crew's adventure and rescue is unlike any other. The Shackleton expedition was one of the most unbelievable struggles for survival in the twentieth century.

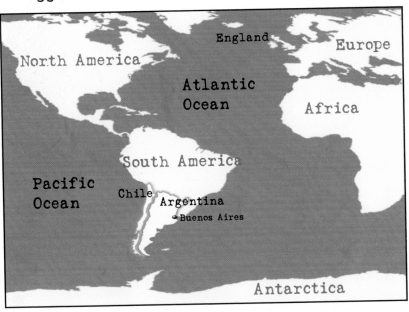

On this map, the red arrow shows the journey that Shackleton had planned. He had hoped to reach Antarctica by way of the Weddell Sea, and then cross the icy continent on foot.

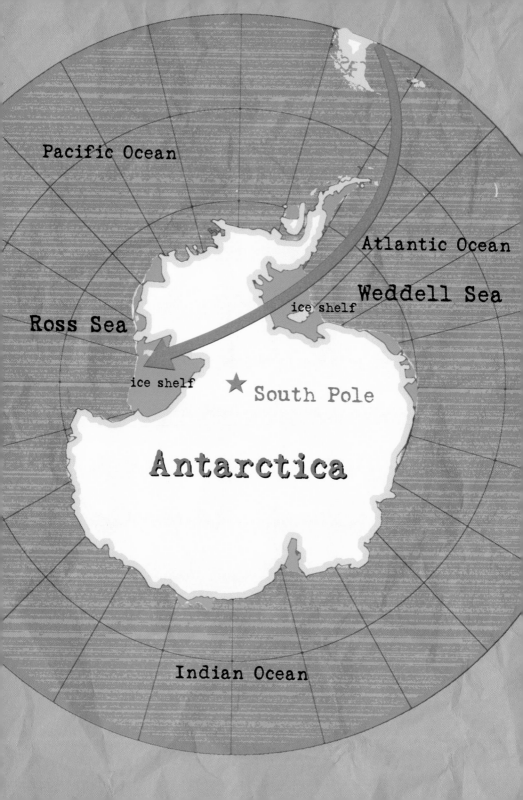

Pacific Ocean

Atlantic Ocean

Weddell Sea

Ross Sea

ice shelf

ice shelf

★ South Pole

Antarctica

Indian Ocean

One

A Chilling Experience

On January 1, 1914, Sir Ernest Shackleton announced his expedition plans. He had bought a ship, the *Endurance*, that was specially built to withstand the ice around Antarctica. He placed ads, inviting people to serve as crew members on his expedition. He would lead his crew through the Atlantic Ocean to Antarctica. Once there, they would walk across the continent.

Hundreds of people applied. Only twenty-seven men were chosen. The selected men left England on August 8, 1914. They sailed the *Endurance* from England to Buenos Aires, Argentina, in South America. Shackleton joined the men there. Also joining the expedition were sixty-nine sled dogs that would help pull the men across Antarctica.

Seven months after announcing his plans, Shackleton's crew set sail in the open seas toward Antarctica.

While in Buenos Aires, three men were kicked out of the crew for fighting. They were quickly replaced. Charles Green, a cook, and William Bakewell, an experienced sailor, were invited to join the expedition. Bakewell's friend Perce Blackborow wanted to join, but Shackleton didn't want anyone else. Still, Blackborow snuck on board the ship, hiding in a clothes locker.

On October 26, the *Endurance* left Buenos Aires for the island of South Georgia, the final stop before Antarctica. One day later, Blackborow was discovered. The men dragged the stowaway to Shackleton. He yelled at Blackborow in front of the crew, but eventually decided to hire him as a steward. The *Endurance* reached South Georgia on November 5.

The crew stayed at Grytviken, a whaling station. Shackleton learned from the whalers that there was an unusually large amount of ice that year. Due to the danger, the crew stayed on South Georgia for a whole month.

Only six weeks after heading out from South Georgia, Shackleton and his crew got stuck in pack ice.

December 5, 1914

The *Endurance* left South Georgia for Antarctica. Only two days later, the ship entered pack ice— great sheets of ice clumped close together. The *Endurance* plowed through until January 19, 1915, when the ship got stuck. There was ice as far as the eye could see. Ice surrounded the *Endurance*. The crew was trapped.

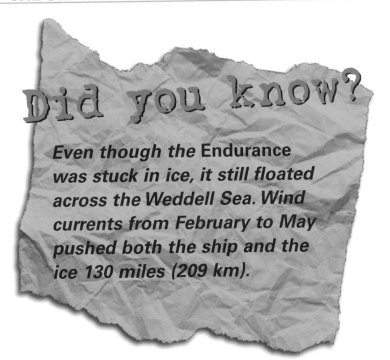

Did you know?

Even though the Endurance was stuck in ice, it still floated across the Weddell Sea. Wind currents from February to May pushed both the ship and the ice 130 miles (209 km).

In the Southern Hemisphere, winter begins in May. By late February, Shackleton finally realized that the *Endurance* would remain stuck in ice through the long winter. The crew moved the dogs off of the ship and built "dogloos" as shelters for them. The crew moved into the ship's storage area for warmth. Making fun of its lack of glamour, they jokingly named their sleeping quarters "the Ritz." The Ritz was made up of

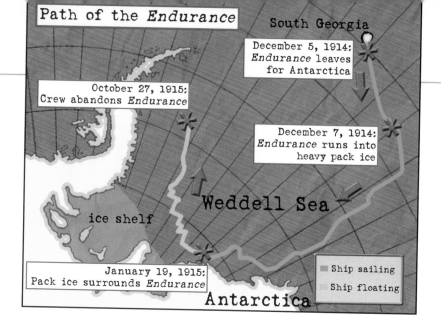

Path of the *Endurance*

South Georgia

December 5, 1914:
Endurance leaves
for Antarctica

October 27, 1915:
Crew abandons *Endurance*

December 7, 1914:
Endurance runs into
heavy pack ice

Weddell Sea

ice shelf

January 19, 1915:
Pack ice surrounds *Endurance*

Ship sailing

Ship floating

Antarctica

eleven cubicles that were each 6 feet by 5 feet.
Two men shared each cubicle.

Cold Comfort

The men found many ways to get through the
boredom of the long days. They cared for the
dogs and read to one another. They sang, played
chess, and listened to records. Another favorite
pastime was playing football on the ice. These
activities helped make the frigid days bearable.

Months passed. Finally, on August 1, the ice
in front of the *Endurance* broke. They were free!
The men hurried to get the dogs on the ship.

Just as the dogs were on board, the ice around the *Endurance* crushed the dogloos. For 15 minutes, the ship floated calmly. Then, as the ice churned beneath it, the *Endurance* became stuck again.

For two months, ice pressed against the ship. On October 24, the pressure of the ice cracked the hull, or body of the ship, and caused a leak. The men worked furiously to bail out the water, but it was useless. Three days later, Shackleton

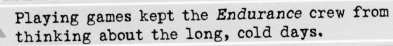 Playing games kept the *Endurance* crew from thinking about the long, cold days.

ordered his crew to abandon the sinking ship. The *Endurance* had lost its battle. From now on, the men would focus all of their energy on making it home alive.

In late October, the crew of the *Endurance* was forced to abandon the sinking ship.

TWO

Stranded on a Frozen Ocean

The nearest place where the crew might find food or shelter was Paulet Island. In 1902, explorers had left supplies on Paulet Island for future adventurers. Paulet Island was 346 miles (557 km) away—the same distance as New York to Pittsburgh.

The men were only allowed to bring 2 pounds of personal items. Frank Hurley, the expedition's photographer, was allowed to carry more. Yet he still had to leave behind many pieces of equipment. The dogs were harnessed to sleds. The men pulled the lifeboats. The loaded lifeboats weighed as much as 1 ton (907 kg). It took fifteen men to pull just one. The three lifeboats were named the *James Caird*, the *Dudley Docker*, and the *Stancomb Wills*.

◄ With three heavy lifeboats to pull behind them, the men soon learned that each step forward would be a struggle.

It was slow going. After three hours, the crew had covered only 1 mile. Exhausted, they set up camp on an ice floe. The next morning, they only traveled three-quarters of a mile before stopping. They named their stopping point "Ocean Camp."

Icy Life

Life at Ocean Camp was hard. Keeping warm was a difficult but crucial task. Each man had a sleeping bag. Some sleeping bags were made of wool. Others were made of warmer reindeer hide. The tents were made of such thin material that the men could see the moon from inside them. It was so cold that the moisture from their breath made a light snow. Much of the food on the *Endurance* had already been eaten. The men had to kill seals, penguins, and any other animals that they could. A normal breakfast was fried seal with "bannocks," or lumps of baked dough, and tea. Dinner was usually "hoosh," or penguin stew, and hot cocoa. Without warning, though,

The *Endurance* photographer, Frank Hurley, captured the severe living conditions of the shipwrecked crew.

the crew could no longer find penguins and seals. The men grew concerned. They had enough food to last for only one hundred days.

December 23, 1915

Two days before Christmas, the crew left Ocean Camp in hopes of finding land. This time, they took only two lifeboats. Many supplies were left behind to lighten the lifeboats. The slushy snow made the going slow. Hungry, tired, and wet, the

men could only march a mile and a half each day. Shackleton decided to find a sturdy floe for a new camp. Some men went back to get more supplies from Ocean Camp. Shackleton ordered them to also bring back the third lifeboat. Many men were relieved by this decision because they did not believe that they would all fit into two lifeboats.

Patience Wears Thin

The men named their new camp "Patience Camp." Life was getting more difficult by the day. Food was scarce and so was blubber, the fat from animals such as seals and penguins. The men used blubber as fuel in their stoves. Without blubber, they would have to eat frozen meat.

The men prepared to sail the lifeboats to land. On March 28, 1916, the ice that Patience Camp rested on split. A major crack ran under the lifeboat *James Caird*. The men hurried to get everything to safety. As they sprang into action,

Shackleton (right) and a crew member prepare a hot meal of hoosh for dinner.

a large shape loomed in the distance. Frank Wild, the second-in-command, grabbed his rifle and shot. The intruder collapsed. When the men reached it, they discovered that it was an 11-foot-long leopard seal. Wild had killed it with one shot. This one animal provided 1,000 pounds (454 kg) of meat. Inside the leopard seal's stomach were fifty fish that the men also ate.

There was no longer a shortage of food or blubber, but the crew still wasn't safe. The ice continued to crack around them. The men could

see the distant peaks of Elephant Island from their camp. They made plans to sail there. The dogs were killed and eaten. On April 9, when the ice broke up, the men launched their boats into the chilly waters.

Elephant Island

The men had spent 170 days floating on the ice. The next week was to be an entirely different challenge. The sea was harsh, the wind high, and the men weak. Each boat was only 22½ feet (6.8 meters) long. As the boats tossed in the churning sea, water poured over their sides and quickly turned to ice. Many men suffered from frostbite.

After seven rough days, the men finally reached Elephant Island. Shackleton wanted Blackborow, the youngest crew member, to be the first on land. When they landed and Blackborow didn't rise from his seat, Shackleton helped him off the boat. Blackborow just fell into the water. His feet were so badly frostbitten that he could

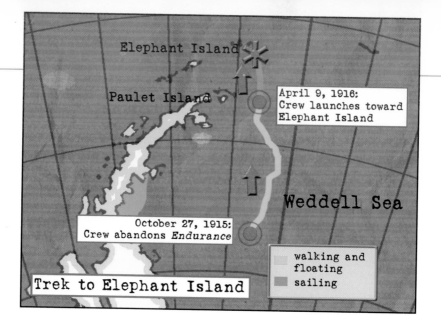

Elephant Island

Paulet Island

April 9, 1916:
Crew launches toward
Elephant Island

Weddell Sea

October 27, 1915:
Crew abandons *Endurance*

walking and
floating
sailing

Trek to Elephant Island

no longer stand. Incredibly, the crew's mood was light. That's because this was the first time any of them had been on land in 497 days.

Elephant Island was not a welcoming place, though. The entire island was only 100 feet (30 m) wide. Wind from the turbulent sea ripped across the island day and night. Everything was blown around constantly. Even the *Dudley Docker*, one of the three half-ton (454 kg) lifeboats, was tossed around by the harsh wind. Shackleton soon decided that their only hope of rescue was to sail the *James Caird* back to South Georgia.

Three

The Impossible Journey

South Georgia was more than 800 miles (1,287 km) from Elephant Island. This was a far greater distance than they had just traveled. Plus, the waters that the crew would have to sail were more dangerous.

Despite this knowledge, almost all of the men wanted to go. Shackleton chose Frank Worsley, Tom Crean, Harry McNeish, John Vincent, and Timothy McCarthy to go with him. Worsley would be the navigator. His job was to figure out the best course for the boat to travel. Crean was chosen mainly because he was a troublemaker. Shackleton didn't want to leave him with the others. The same was true for Vincent and McNeish. However, Vincent was much stronger than the other men, and McNeish was a very

◄ The winds on Elephant Island were strong enough to toss the massive lifeboats as if they were toys.

skilled woodworker. This skill would come in handy if repairs were needed on the *James Caird*. Finally, Shackleton chose McCarthy because of his experience and strength.

Voyage of the *James Caird*

McNeish worked on the *James Caird*, raising the sides of the lifeboat so that it would be more seaworthy. He did this by nailing up boards that the crew had taken from the *Endurance*. After McNeish finished, the *James Caird* was loaded up with supplies. The men brought enough food to last four weeks. If they did not make it to land by then, they would be lost at sea.

On April 24, 1916, the six men left Elephant Island for South Georgia, eighteen months after they had first set out for it. The men had to sail through the Bransfield Strait. The Bransfield Strait is difficult for large boats to navigate, let alone an open, 22½-foot-long

 Shackleton and five other men launched the *James Caird* in a desperate attempt to find help.

(6.9 m) lifeboat. Winds of 80 miles (129 km) per hour crashed against the boat. Waves rose as high as 60 feet (18 m).

As the *James Caird* made its way to South Georgia, ice from the waves rocked against the little boat. At one point, the lifeboat's entire hull had a crust of ice that was 15 inches (38.1 cm) thick. The men had to chip off the ice to keep the boat from sinking. This was a difficult and dangerous task. The men clung to the slick boat and chipped the ice at the same time.

Sick from the tossing sea, frostbitten, and weary, the men were about to collapse. Shackleton did all he could to keep them going. During the day, hot meals were served every four hours. At night, the men drank hot milk to keep warm.

Worsley tried to figure out where they were. Cloudy skies made it difficult for him to get a good reading from the sextant. A sextant is a device that measures the angles between objects. It aids sailors and helps them navigate the open sea. Using a sextant in bad weather is hard, though. The center of the sun must be lined up with the horizon in the eyepiece of the sextant.

If the sun is behind clouds or fog, the exact center is difficult to find. South Georgia is 100 miles (161 km) long, but only 25 miles (40 km) wide. If the reading was off by even a little bit, the crew would miss the island completely. Then they would veer hopelessly off course.

The voyage was also extremely uncomfortable. The boat had a low piece of canvas that sheltered the men from the constant splashing of waves. Still, water poured in from every direction, soaking the crew to the skin. None of the men could sit upright under the canvas. They had to lie down while they ate. Their sleeping bags had rotted and were now shedding reindeer hair. The hair sometimes choked the men while they slept. Worse, the only remaining fresh water was now filled with reindeer hair and salty ocean water that had spilled over the side. If the men didn't find land soon, they would die.

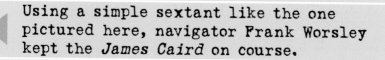

Using a simple sextant like the one pictured here, navigator Frank Worsley kept the *James Caird* on course.

Land, Ho!

At about half past noon on May 9, McCarthy spotted South Georgia! The men were about 10 miles (16 km) out. As they neared the island, it became apparent that they could not safely reach the island from where they were. Their boat would smash into the large rocks and cliffs along the shore. They decided to wait until morning to try to find a better place to land.

That night, a hurricane hit. Powerful winds blew them toward the island's deadly cliffs. The men were able to turn the boat away, only to be blown into the cliffs of a nearby island.

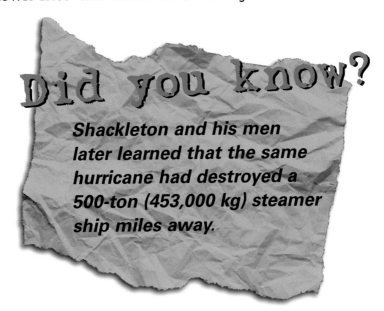

Did you know?

Shackleton and his men later learned that the same hurricane had destroyed a 500-ton (453,000 kg) steamer ship miles away.

Nine hours later, the winds finally died down. After many tries, the men managed to steer the boat into a small harbor on the island. The exhausted men tied up their boat. They had finally made it to South Georgia—two weeks after they had started out. Yet their journey was not over.

Jagged Journey South

Shackleton and his crew had landed on the south side of South Georgia. Unfortunately, the island's only human inhabitants lived on the north side. The *James Caird* had been damaged by the storm. Sailing it around the island would be impossible. The men would have to cross it by foot, something no one had ever done before.

The mountains were steep and jagged. Glaciers and cliffs fell sharply into the ocean. Shackleton and his men were tired, hungry, and did not have proper mountain climbing equipment. Still, their lives and twenty-two

others depended on getting across these mountains. Shackleton decided he would attempt the crossing with Worsley and Crean. The others were to wait for rescue. The three men spent the next few days preparing. The only supplies they would carry would be food for three days, two compasses, 50 feet (15.2 m) of rope, and a carpenter's adze to use as an ice pick. They could not even carry sleeping bags or tents.

On May 19, the three men set off for the island's north side. They met many steep inclines and dead ends. Shackleton thought he heard a whistle on the morning of May 21. If it had come

from the whaling station on South Georgia, it would go off again in a half hour, to start the whalers' working day. The men waited. At 7:00 A.M., the whistle went off again. This was the first sound from civilization that the men had heard for seventeen months!

Return to Civilization

It was now 4:00 P.M. The men at the whaling station had just finished working. Two young boys saw the ragged men first. Shackleton, Worsley, and Crean were covered in dirt. Their clothes were worn out and their hair and beards were overgrown and stiff. The boys ran away from them. Then the foreman of the whaling station came to meet the men. Shackleton asked to be taken to the whaling station's manager, Thoralf Sørrle. Sørrle was astonished that Shackleton and his men had even survived. He took them in for showers and shaves.

Even though they arrived on the wrong side of the island, South Georgia was a welcome sight to the *James Caird* crew.

Four

Operation: Rescue!

That night, Worsley went with a crew of whalers to rescue McNeish, Vincent, and McCarthy. The three men did not recognize Worsley. They had not seen him clean and shaven in seventeen months.

Almost immediately, Shackleton began making plans to rescue his crew left on Elephant Island. On May 23, two days after arriving at the whaling station, he set out on the *Southern Sky* to Elephant Island. But after ten days, he returned. The boat could not get closer than 60 miles (97 km) from the island. The ice was too thick. His next two tries also failed to reach the island. However, Shackleton did not give up.

The government of England promised to send another ship, the *Discovery*, to assist with the rescue. However, *Discovery* wouldn't be ready to sail

Although exhausted, Sir Shackleton refused to rest. Soon after reaching the whaling station, he set off to rescue the rest of his crew.

until October. Shackleton refused to wait that long. He asked the Chilean government for help. Chile was the closest nation that could offer assistance. Chilean officials agreed to lend him the *Yelcho*, a small boat made out of steel. On August 25, the *Yelcho* left South Georgia. The *Yelcho* reached Elephant Island on August 30, 1916, four months after Shackleton and his crew of five had left.

Stranded on Elephant Island

Meanwhile, back on Elephant Island, conditions were severe. Fierce winds blew across the little piece of land. The tents were not fit for this weather. At first, the men tried to sleep in caves they dug in the ice. However, the ice melted from the men's body heat and made everything wet. The men then built a shelter out of the lifeboats and tents. They turned the boats upside down and laid them on rock walls that the men had made. The tents were then put around the

With each day, the men on Elephant Island grew weaker. Yet they never gave up hope.

bottom of the boats to shield the men from the wind. All twenty-two men slept in the little hut. The crew named the hut the "Snuggery."

There also wasn't much food. To survive, the men had to catch eleven penguins a day. About 1,300 penguins were eaten while the men were on Elephant Island.

As the weeks passed, hope began to fade. The men knew that Shackleton and the five others had only taken enough food for four weeks. They expected to see a rescue ship sometime in June or July. June and July passed. Still, there was no ship. The men began to worry. What if the *James*

Caird didn't make it? What could they do?

A desperate plan was made to send another group in one of the remaining lifeboats. Because all of their best equipment was with Shackleton, this would be even more dangerous than the trip the *James Caird* had made. Still, they were running low on strength and faith, and this seemed like their last chance.

Salvation!

However, on August 30, crew member George Marston spotted a ship! He ran into the Snuggery and told everyone what he saw. The men tore out of the hut, some without shoes on their feet. Food spilled all over the ground. The doors to the hut were destroyed. There, in the distance, was the *Yelcho*. It was no illusion, no dream. The men were saved!

On the *Yelcho*, Shackleton scanned the island with his binoculars. He counted the men as they jumped and waved on the beach. All twenty-two

The *Yelcho* was a sight for sore eyes. Shackleton and his crew knew that their two years of frustration were nearly over.

were there! Everyone was still alive. In one hour, the men were on their way back to South Georgia, safe at last.

The reunion of all twenty-eight men represented a joyous end to a terrifying journey. They had battled horrible conditions to make it back alive. The Shackleton Expedition is a lasting tribute to human courage and endurance.

adze an ax-like tool

bannocks lumps of baked dough

canvas a strong, heavy cloth made of cotton

climate the kind of weather a place has

expedition a long trip for a special purpose

floe a large sheet of floating ice

frostbite an injury to a part of the body caused by freezing temperatures

glaciers great masses of ice that move slowly down mountains

hoosh penguin stew

hurricane a fierce storm with strong winds and very heavy rains

inhabitants residents

navigator the person in charge of steering or guiding a ship

sextant an instrument used to find latitude and longitude at sea

steward the person on a ship who is responsible for the comfort of the passengers

stowaway someone who hides on a ship to get a free ride

whalers people who hunt whales

Armstrong, Jennifer. *Shipwreck at the Bottom of the World: The Extraordinary True Story of Shackleton and the* Endurance. New York: Random House, 2000.

Hooper, Meredith. *The* Endurance: *Shackleton's Perilous Expedition in Antarctica.* New York: Abbeville Press, 2001.

Kimmel, Elizabeth Cody. *Ice Story: Shackleton's Lost Expedition.* New York: Houghton Mifflin Company, 1999.

Kostyal, K. M. and Alexandra Shackleton. *Trial by Ice: A Photobiography of Sir Ernest Shackleton*. Washington, D.C.: National Geographic Society, 1999.

Kulling, Monica. *Sea of Ice: The Wreck of the Endurance*. New York: Random House, 1999.

McCurdy, Michael. *Trapped by the Ice!: Shackleton's Amazing Antarctic Adventure*. New York: Walker Publishing Company, 1997.

RESOURCES

WEB SITES
Shackleton's Antarctic Odyssey
http://www.pbs.org/wgbh/nova/shackleton/
This site has a detailed account of Shackleton's expedition. You can also read about three men who reenacted Shackleton's journey across the mountains of South Georgia.

Endurance: Shackleton's Legendary Antarctic Expedition
http://www.amnh.org/exhibitions/shackleton/
  expedintro.html
This Web site is sponsored by the American Museum of Natural History. Read all about the voyage and see some incredible pictures taken by the expedition's photographer, Frank Hurley.

Kodak: The *Endurance*

http://www.kodak.com/US/en/corp/
    features/endurance/

Kodak provided film and equipment to Frank Hurley. See his amazing photographs and read about Shackleton's adventures on this Web site.

ORGANIZATIONS

Royal Geographic Society
1 Kensington Gore
London SW7 2AR
United Kingdom
Email: info@rgs.org

The Antarctica Project
1630 Connecticut Ave., N.W., 3rd floor
Washington, D.C. 20009
Tel: (202) 234-2480
Email: antarctica@igc.org

INDEX

INDEX

About the Author

Jil Fine is an editor and freelance writer living in Brooklyn, New York. She enjoys an occasional adventure.